DOUBLE ASTEROID REDIRECTION TEST

Defending Earth from Asteroids

Diane Bailey

Lerner Publications ◆ Minneapolis

Lerner Publications Company
An imprint of Lerner Publishing Group, Inc.
241 First Avenue North
Minneapolis, MN 55401 USA

For reading levels and more information, look up this title at www.lernerbooks.com.

Main body text set in Aptifer Sans Regular.
Typeface provided by Linotype.

Library of Congress Cataloging-in-Publication Data

Names: Bailey, Diane, 1966–author.
Title: Double Asteroid Redirection Test : defending Earth from asteroids / Diane Bailey.
Description: Minneapolis, MN : Lerner Publications, [2024] | Series: Space explorer guidebooks (Alternator books) | Includes bibliographical references and index. | Audience: Ages 8–12 | Audience: Grades 4–6 | Summary: "Asteroids are always moving in space, but what do we do if one of these giant space rocks heads straight for Earth? With technology and spacecrafts like DART, we now have the answer"—Provided by publisher.
Identifiers: LCCN 2023011301 (print) | LCCN 2023011302 (ebook) | ISBN 9798765609088 (library binding) | ISBN 9798765624937 (paperback) | ISBN 9798765617786 (epub) |
Subjects: LCSH: Double Asteroid Redirection Test (Spacecraft)—Juvenile literature. | Asteroids—Juvenile literature. | BISAC: JUVENILE NONFICTION / Science & Nature / Astronomy
Classification: LCC QB651 .B32 2024 (print) | LCC QB651 (ebook) | DDC 523.44—dc23/ eng20230714

LC record available at https://lccn.loc.gov/2023011301
LC ebook record available at https://lccn.loc.gov/2023011302

Manufactured in the United States of America
1 – CG – 12/15/23

TABLE OF CONTENTS

INTRODUCTION

GET OUT OF THE WAY!

On September 26, 2022, the video screens at the National Aeronautics and Space Agency (NASA) went dark. The signal from the agency's Double Asteroid Redirection Test (DART) spacecraft

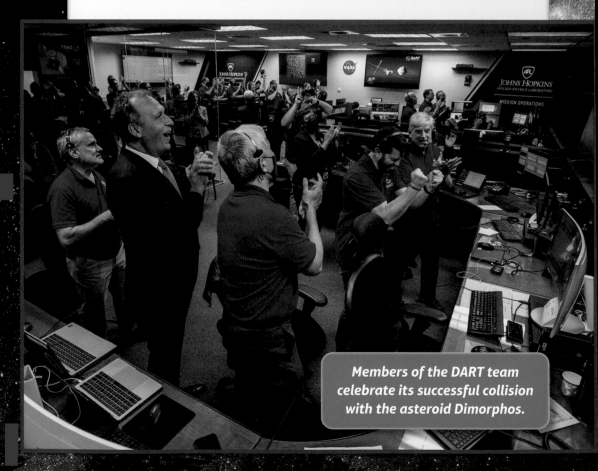

Members of the DART team celebrate its successful collision with the asteroid Dimorphos.

The DART spacecraft is comparable in size to a vending machine.

had been lost. The people watching knew what this meant: DART had crashed into an asteroid. It was destroyed.

So why was everybody cheering? Because NASA didn't want their spacecraft back. Instead, smashing it to smithereens was the test of a bold idea. They hoped the force from the impact would be strong enough to shove the asteroid out of its orbit— and that's exactly what happened!

At first glance, DART was even more successful than expected. The big question now is: Can DART successfully defend Earth from asteroids that get too close?

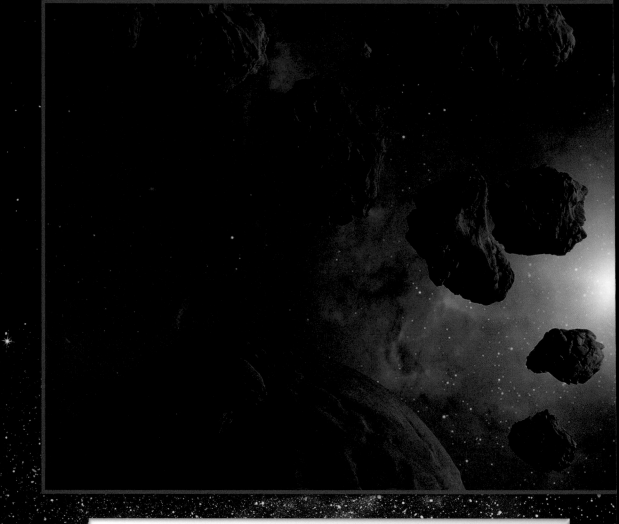

CHAPTER 1

IMPACT!

Scientists estimate that between 80 and 100 tons (73 and 91 metric tons) of space stuff falls on the planet every day, but

Asteroids and debris create clutter in space.

you probably don't even notice it. Most of it is just dust or small meteors, pieces of asteroids that burn up as they pass through Earth's atmosphere. Sometimes this stuff makes impressive light shows in the sky, but it doesn't do much damage. Occasionally, though, a bigger piece makes its way through to Earth's surface. Most of the known asteroids orbit within the asteroid belt between Mars and Jupiter.

ROCK AND ROLL

A huge asteroid hit the Earth sixty-five million years ago. Scientists think it was at least six miles (9.7 km) across, maybe more. It crashed in what is now Mexico, causing extreme devastation. Rocks were vaporized in the blast, letting loose chemicals into the atmosphere that caused acid rain. Clouds of debris blocked out the sunlight for months. The temperature plummeted and plants stopped growing. Many of Earth's life forms, including dinosaurs, went extinct.

An impact large enough to harm the whole planet happens only once in millions of years, but smaller ones can still cause damage. In 1908, people living in the Tunguska region of Russia heard a loud boom one morning. Some thought an alien spacecraft had exploded in the sky. Earth was being invaded— but not by aliens. It was a 120-foot (37 m) meteorite! The blast caused intense heat and shock waves and killed millions of trees.

One theory about dinosaur extinction is that they were wiped out by asteroids.

Scientists estimate that the Barringer Meteor Crater was caused by the impact of an asteroid about 150 feet (46 m) wide over fifty thousand years ago.

KEEPING WATCH

The pressure from a large asteroid impact can flatten trees and buildings. The heat can spark wildfires. The shock can trigger earthquakes. Scientists want to know about possible strikes before they happen, so they can warn people.

How do they know if an asteroid is a danger? Like Earth, asteroids orbit the Sun. Most of them are in the asteroid belt between Mars and Jupiter, and don't come near Earth. However, all things are affected by gravity, a force that attracts objects with mass toward one another. The greater the mass, the stronger the gravity. Asteroids can be pulled off course by an object with a large mass, like Jupiter or even a bigger asteroid. That could put them on a new path that intersects with Earth's orbit.

Earth can't jump out of the way, but scientists have some ideas for defending the planet. That's what DART is all about.

The brightest sets of orange dots belong to asteroids Klotho and Lina.

CHAPTER 2

JOURNEY TO AN ASTEROID

Think about playing pool. If you hit one ball into another ball, the force pushes the second ball away. That's called kinetic impact.

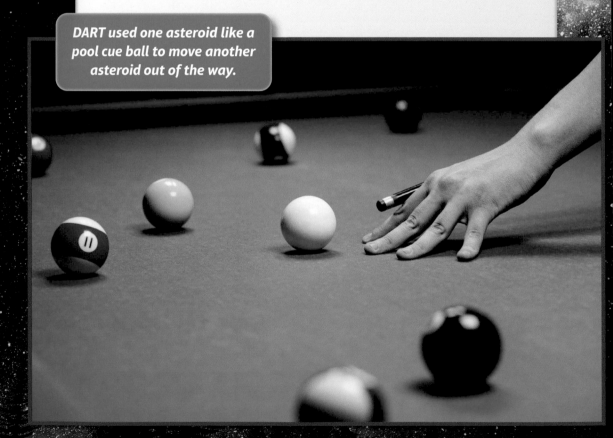

DART used one asteroid like a pool cue ball to move another asteroid out of the way.

This diagram shows the plan to use images from powerful telescopes to navigate the DART spacecraft to its intended target.

DART worked the same way. It darted millions of miles to crash into an asteroid and push it out of its orbit.

SEEING DOUBLE

The D in DART stands for "double." That's because scientists chose a pair of asteroids, Didymos and Dimorphos, for the test. The asteroids are about 7 million miles (11.3 million km) away from Earth and weren't a threat. NASA chose them because their orbit brought them fairly close to Earth in 2022, and because they are easy to observe through telescopes.

An asteroid like Dimorphos is relatively small compared to the largest known asteroid which is about 329 miles (530 km) in diameter.

Dimorphos, the smaller asteroid, orbits the larger one, Didymos. Dimorphos was NASA's target. It takes just under twelve hours to complete one orbit around Didymos. NASA wanted to shove it a little closer to Didymos, to make its orbit shorter. If Dimorphos had been a threat, the change in its orbit would have been enough to protect Earth.

Scientists faced a lot of technical challenges. They used computers to model how the DART test would work, but there

was a lot they didn't know. What was Dimorphos made of? How massive was it? Without those answers, it was hard to predict whether DART would succeed. Also, Dimorphos is only about 525 feet (160 m) across—roughly the length of one and a half football fields. With even the tiniest wrong turn, DART would miss it. Could NASA do it? There was only one way to find out.

Who knew the results would be so surprising!

DART was launched on a SpaceX Falcon 9 rocket from the Vandenberg Space Force Base in California.

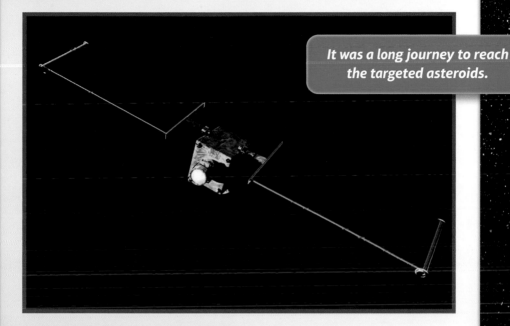

It was a long journey to reach the targeted asteroids.

GETTING THERE

DART was launched on November 23, 2021. It traveled peacefully for about ten months before reaching Didymos and Dimorphos. In the last few hours of the trip, the asteroids appeared on DART's onboard camera. Then, the real excitement began.

DART was about the size of a vending machine and was packed with advanced technology. It used an automatic navigation system, like those on self-driving cars. That helped it steer toward Dimorphos. DART's camera snapped pictures as it hurtled toward the asteroid at almost 15,000 miles (24,140 km) per hour, or 4 miles (6 km) per second. Scientists at NASA could see individual rocks on the surface of Dimorphos . . . until everything went black. That's when the cheering started.

A close-up image of Dimorphos taken just before impact revealed it to have a rubble pile structure.

CHAPTER 3

NEW DISCOVERIES

DART worked even better than NASA had hoped. Their goal had been to make the orbit of Dimorphos about ten minutes shorter. They actually cut it by more than half an hour! It turned out that DART had gotten a little help from the asteroid itself.

AN EXTRA PUSH

A special probe separated from DART about two weeks before the crash to get pictures of the impact. Those images showed a huge plume of ejecta, more than 10,000 miles (16,093 km) long. It was made of material that shot up from the surface of Dimorphos after the impact.

The Hubble Space Telescope images show plumes of ejecta expanding over time after DART impacted Dimorphos.

+22 minutes

+5 hours

+8.2 hours

Dimorphos just eleven seconds before impact.

Imagine holding a balloon filled with air. Let go and the air whooshes out. The balloon shoots away in the opposite direction from the air being released. In this case, the ejecta was like the released air. The asteroid shot away in the opposite direction. This increased the force of DART's impact by about 3.5 times, making the asteroid move farther.

SOLID OR SQUISHY?

Some asteroids are solid chunks of rock. Others are composed of many smaller, individual rocks held together by their own gravity. In recent years, more and more rubble-pile asteroids have been discovered. They are more common than we originally thought. That's both good and bad.

Nancy Chabot

Nancy Chabot was a science fiction fan when she was a kid. She loved watching *Star Wars* and was fascinated by the idea of different worlds: planets with two suns, people living in clouds. She decided to become a planetary scientist to explore more. Now, she studies how rocky planets and asteroids are formed and how they change over time. She is also a leader of the DART team. Missions like this one are a dream come true for her.

Planetary scientist Nancy Chabot's search for meteorites has taken her to Antarctica several times.

COUNT THEM UP

Astronomers are busy looking for all the asteroids within about 30 million miles (48 million km) of Earth. So far, they've found about twenty-six thousand. About ten thousand of those are more than 460 feet (140 m) across—large enough to cause a lot of damage if they strike Earth. We're not in danger from anything we know of, but scientists believe there are about fifteen thousand more large asteroids they haven't found yet.

Rubble-pile asteroids are like squishy pillows. If something hits them, they act like large shock absorbers. The force won't push them as far. That's bad. However, there is space between all the pieces. That makes them less massive and dense, so they

Hubble

Webb

Images of DART taken by the Hubble and James Webb Space Telescopes just moments before impact

don't need as much force to make them move. Also, they produce more ejecta, which gives that extra push. That's good. Because of the large amount of ejecta photographed, scientists think Dimorphos is a rubble-pile asteroid.

Preparing DART for its planetary defense mission

CHAPTER 4

DEFENDING THE PLANET

DART was only the first step in the Dimorphos mission. The next step is to find out more about the asteroid itself. Scientists hope this data will make as much impact as the crash itself.

THE HERA MISSION

The European Space Agency (ESA) has scheduled another spacecraft, Hera, to arrive at Dimorphos in December 2026. There's no big hurry. The ejecta DART threw up made quite a mess, making it hard to get good pictures. By the time Hera arrives, a lot of that will have settled, making it easier to see.

Hera will study the crater DART made. That will help scientists understand more about Dimorphos. How massive is it? What is it made of? Squishier asteroids can change shape if they're struck hard enough. Did that happen to Dimorphos? Researchers are looking forward to getting more detailed data.

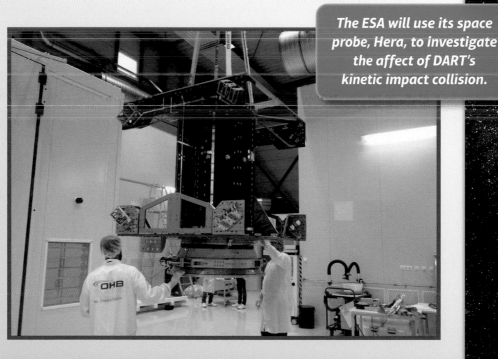

The ESA will use its space probe, Hera, to investigate the affect of DART's kinetic impact collision.

GRAVITY TRACTOR

If asteroids are spotted early, a gravity tractor could fly alongside it for years and slowly pull it out of Earth's path.

DIFFERENT APPROACHES

The kinetic impact method used by DART is not the only possible way to move an asteroid. A gravity tractor spacecraft is still just an idea, but it might be built one day. It would travel to an asteroid and stop nearby. The massive tractor would have its own gravity, and over time it would act like a tugboat, slowly pulling the asteroid off course.

Another idea is to vaporize part of the surface of the asteroid, using a nuclear explosive or possibly lasers. That would also create a plume of ejecta that could change the asteroid's path.

Other ideas include using mirrors to focus destructive solar energy on an asteroid or firing projectiles at it. Experts are trying to figure out which ideas work and which ones don't.

DON'T BLOW IT

Shattering an asteroid using explosives isn't a good idea. For one thing, it's less efficient than just using a big spacecraft. Spacecraft travel so fast that they create more force than explosives. Also, breaking up an asteroid just makes more pieces. They still travel in the same direction, meaning more possible impacts.

In 2020, an SUV-sized asteroid named "OG" was spotted closer to Earth than any non-impacting asteroid ever detected.

How about some space graffiti? The surface of an asteroid absorbs sunlight and converts it to heat. At night the surface cools and releases the heat as tiny particles. Those particles make a tiny ejecta plume that still makes a tiny thrust. It's not much, but it adds up over time. Not all surfaces work the same way, though. Darker surfaces tend to absorb light, while lighter ones reflect it. That changes the amount of thrust. Scientists have suggested spray-painting one side of an asteroid white to change the thrust level and knock the asteroid off balance.

Defending the planet is a big job, and astronomers are always scanning the skies to keep Earth safe. They find new asteroids all the time—and they're also finding new ways to push them out of Earth's path.

The majority of known asteroids are too far away to be a danger to Earth.

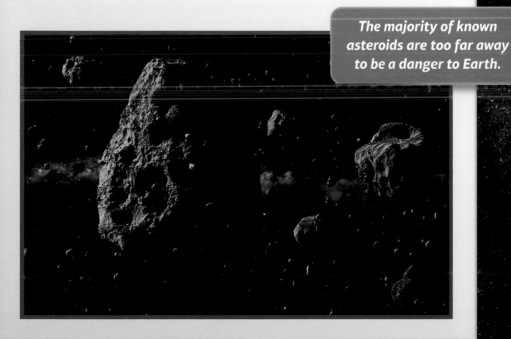

GLOSSARY

asteroid belt: the area between Mars and Jupiter where most asteroids in our solar system are located

ejecta: material that is thrown outward as the result of an impact

gravity: the force that attracts objects with mass toward one another

kinetic impact: the force transferred by a moving object when it collides with another object

mass: the amount of matter an object has

orbit: the repeating path of an object in space moving around another object

plume: a cloud of smoke or debris that resembles the shape of a feather

probe: a device used to send back information especially from outer space

thrust: a force that propels, or pushes, an object

vaporize: to turn a solid or liquid into a gas

LEARN MORE

Dickmann, Nancy. *Chasing Comets, Asteroids, and Mysterious Space Objects*. New York: Crabtree Publishing, 2019.

Kenney, Karen Latchana. *Breakthroughs in Planet and Comet Research*. Minneapolis: Lerner Publications, 2019.

Kiddle: Asteroid Facts for Kids
https://kids.kiddle.co/Asteroid

The Kids Should See This: ESA's Incredible Adventures of the Hera Asteroid Mission
https://thekidshouldseethis.com/post/esa-hera-asteroid-mission-animation

NASA Knows: For Students
https://www.nasa.gov/audience/forstudents/5-8/features/nasa-knows/index.html

Reichley, Lisa. *Our Solar System: An Exploration of Planets, Moons, Asteroids, and Other Mysteries of Space*. Emeryville, CA: Rockridge Press, 2020.

Space Place
https://spaceplace.nasa.gov

Wilberforce, Bert. Comets, *Asteroids, and Meteoroids*. New York: Gareth Stevens, 2021.

INDEX

PHOTO ACKNOWLEDGMENTS

page 4; NASA/David C. Bowman, page 5; Shutterstock/joshimerbin, page 6-7; iStockphoto/Naeblys, page 8; iStockphoto/ratpack223, page 9; iStockphoto/estt, page 10; NASA, page 11; NASA/JPL-Caltech/UCLA, page 12; Shutterstock/Kucher Serhii, page 13; NASA/Johns Hopkins Applied Physics Laboratory, page 14-15; iStockphoto/Aksonov, page 16; NASA/Bill Ingalls, page 17; NASA/JHUAPL, page 18; NASA, page 19; NASA, ESA, Jian-Yang Li (PSI), Alyssa Pagan (STScI), page 20; NASA/Johns Hopkins APL, page 21; Antarctic Search for Meteorites Program/Nancy Chabot, page 22; NASA, page 23; NASA/Johns Hopkins APL/Ed Whitman, page 24; NASA/ESA/OSB, page 25; NASA Photo/Tony Landis, page 26; NASA, page 27; iStockphoto/estt, page 28; NASA/JPL-Caltech, page 29; dottedhippo.

Cover (image): iStock photo/dzika_mrowka
Cover (background): Shutterstock/Maria Starovoytova
Interior background: Shuttesrstock/Sergey Nivens